WILD GARLIC RECIPES

Designed, Typeset and Published by Eileithyia Design 2020

© Eleanor Hayes 2020

This book is sold subject to the condition that it shall not, by way of any trade or otherwise, be lent, resold, hired out, or otherwise circulated without the publisher's prior consent in any form of binding or cover other than that in which it is published.

Eleanor Hayes asserts the moral right to be identified as the author of this work.

First published in Great Britain 2020 by Eielithyia Design.

Image credits

Cover - Familiar wild flowers figured and described by F. Edward Hulme ... 1st- ser, Biodiversity Heritage Library. https://www.biodiversitylibrary.org/page/17796279

p. 2 - A new British flora; London, Gresham Pub. Co.,1919.. biodiversitylibrary.org/page/11453067

p. 5 (top) - Flora von Deutschland, Österreich und der Schweiz Gera,Zezschwitz,1903-. biodiversitylibrary.org/page/12306640 Lords and Ladies illustration - Arum maculatum illustrated by Johann Georg Sturm (Painter: Jacob Sturm)

p. 5 (bottom) - Lords &b Ladies photo - cc-by-sa/2.0 - © Evelyn Simak - geograph.org.uk/p/5376618

All other photos © Eleanor Hayes 2020

WILD GARLIC RECIPES

A COOKBOOK FOR SPRING FORAGERS

Contents

CONDIMENTS 7

Wild Garlic Oil   8
Wild Garlic Butter   9
Wild Garlic Mayonnaise   10
Wild Garlic Vinegar   11
Wild Garlic Garnish   13
Pickled Wild Garlic Flower Heads & Seed Pods   14
Wild Garlic Salad Dressing Vinaigrette   16

SAUCES 19

Wild Garlic Pesto   21
Wild Garlic Salsa   24
Wild Garlic Salsa Verde   26
Wild Garlic Guacamole   27
Wild Garlic Hummus 28
Wild Garlic Dip   29

COLD DISHES 31

Wild Garlic Bread   33
Wild Garlic & Egg Mayo Sandwiches   35
Other Sandwich Ideas 37
Wild Garlic Devilled Eggs   38
Potato Salad with Wild Garlic   39
Wild Garlic Light Salad   40
Wild Garlic Heavy Salad   41

HOT DISHES 43

Wild Garlic & Mushroom Pancakes 44
Wild Garlic & Blue Cheese Pancakes 46
Wild Garlic Soup 47
Wild Garlic Omelette 49
Wild Garlic Scrambled Egg 51
Wild Garlic Coddled Eggs with Cheese 53
Wild Garlic Heuvos Rancheros 54
Jacket Potato with Wilted Wild Garlic & Nutmeg 56
Rik's Wild Garlic & Fried Egg Sandwich 57
Spaghetti & Wild Garlic Pesto 59
Baked Salmon with Wild Garlic Pesto Rice 60
Wild Garlic Risotto 62

INDEX 65

Introduction

I was first introduced to the delights of wild garlic on holiday in the Isle of Wight in the UK.

It was a beautiful May holiday and our friends showed us how delicious and versatile this virulent weed is.

We enjoyed foraging it from the garden and countryside around the cottage; it literally grew in every nook and cranny from underneath hedgerows, in ditches, out in open fields and snuggled into dappled woods.

We enjoyed it cooked and raw and in the end, would just sprinkle chopped wild garlic on just about every meal we had!

On our arrival back in Berkshire we were disappointed to discover there was no wild garlic to be found, despite apparently being a rampant pest in many a garden.

On moving to Somerset in 2018 we were thrilled to discover that here was the home of wild garlic!

It was growing by the sides of public footpaths, in woods on fields – frankly the locals couldn't understand our delight!

Wild garlic is a spring seasonal plant acros much of the Northern hemisphere. Its lush dark green leaves from small bulbs in clumps appear usually underneath trees or in sheltered spots. During its 2 month cycle it sprouts single stems with pretty white flowers in globes forms – much like many other plants of the alium family – and these flowers turn into tiny green globes from which the seeds form, self-seeding itself mercilessly everywhere.

As the bulbs return annually and the seeds spread this pretty plant all over the place so if you can find one wild garlic patch, another is sure to be nearby.

The leaves take an elongated form are pointed at the end and usually grow up to around 20cm in length in small clumps around the side of a hand span.

The flower stems rise above the mat of greenery and stand some 10-20 cm taller than the foliage.

Unlike the strong garlic bulb that we associate with garlic, the only part of the wild garlic we DON'T eat is the bulb. Rather we munch on the tender leaves and stems, the flowers and even the seed pods.

The taste is unmistakably garlicky, and yet there is a grassy, earthy and more delicate nuance to the flavour.

By the end of the season when the flowers have turned to seed, the leaves toughen somewhat and start to lose their flavour.

By the end of May they are a distance aftertaste and one must wait until March the following year in order to enjoy their delights.

Note that it is illegal in the UK to dig up wild garlic bulbs, or forage it from private land. It is also very important to be sure that you are picking the right leaf as there are a few others that grow at the same time that are toxic so forage it with care.

IDENTIFYING WILD GARLIC

Once you are familiar with wild garlic it is almost (but not quite) unmistakeable.

It can be found usually in open, broad-leafed woodland, although is also happy growing on banks, by streams, and where live in Somerset, UK, it pretty much grows everywhere!

It starts to emerge from the earth during the early spring – around the same time as crocuses and early daffodils and its dark green pointy leaves poke out from the ground.

The leaves are long and pointy and grow from a stem that is white near the base. Once the plant has grown fully it sends up flower fronds that initially look like a pointy white bud – up to 2cm in length – contained within a thin membrane.

The mebrane erupts allowing the individual flower stems free in a formation similar to a dandelioin or any other flower from the alium (onion) family. It forms a sphere of small stalks each with a flower on the end.

The flowers themselves have delicate white petals and after the petals fall the flower turns into a small seed pod that looks like 3 tiny balls squeezed together.

You can pick and eat wild garlic from the first moment the leaves appear. Fresh young leaves are peppery with a really garlicky tang. This wanes slightly as the plant matures.

The flowers, stems and seed pods all have their own garlicky flavour – as well as an incredible scent.

Once the plant has flowered the leaves still have a garlicky tang, but they tend to get a bit old and tough and are really past their best, although still better than no wild garlic!

A WORD OF CAUTION

There is a similar-ish plant that grows in very similar places and at similar time of year in the UK to wild garlic called Lords and Ladies (Latin name: Arum Maculate).

It is important to familiarise yourself with this plant as it is toxic (particularly the red berries) and must not be confused with wild garlic.

In fact, when you directly compare the plants their differences are obvious but as they are very often found growing in among the wild garlic, it is very important to ensure you check every single leaf that you collect.

Lords and ladies are characterised by rounder leaves with a wider heart-shape. Their stems are thick like a bluebell and their flowers are like a peace lily and the seed pods are bright red/orange balls.

The best way to judge if you are not sure is to rip the leaf and smell it. If it doesn't smell of garlic, then discard it.

Do not eat any leaf unless you are CERTAIN that you have identified it correctly.

A NOTE ON THE RECIPES

Precise quantities are not something to worry too much about. It will very much depend on how much wild garlic you have and how strong you like it. My estimate is that a good handful is around 30g but your hands may be bigger or smaller so feel free to adapt as you see fit.

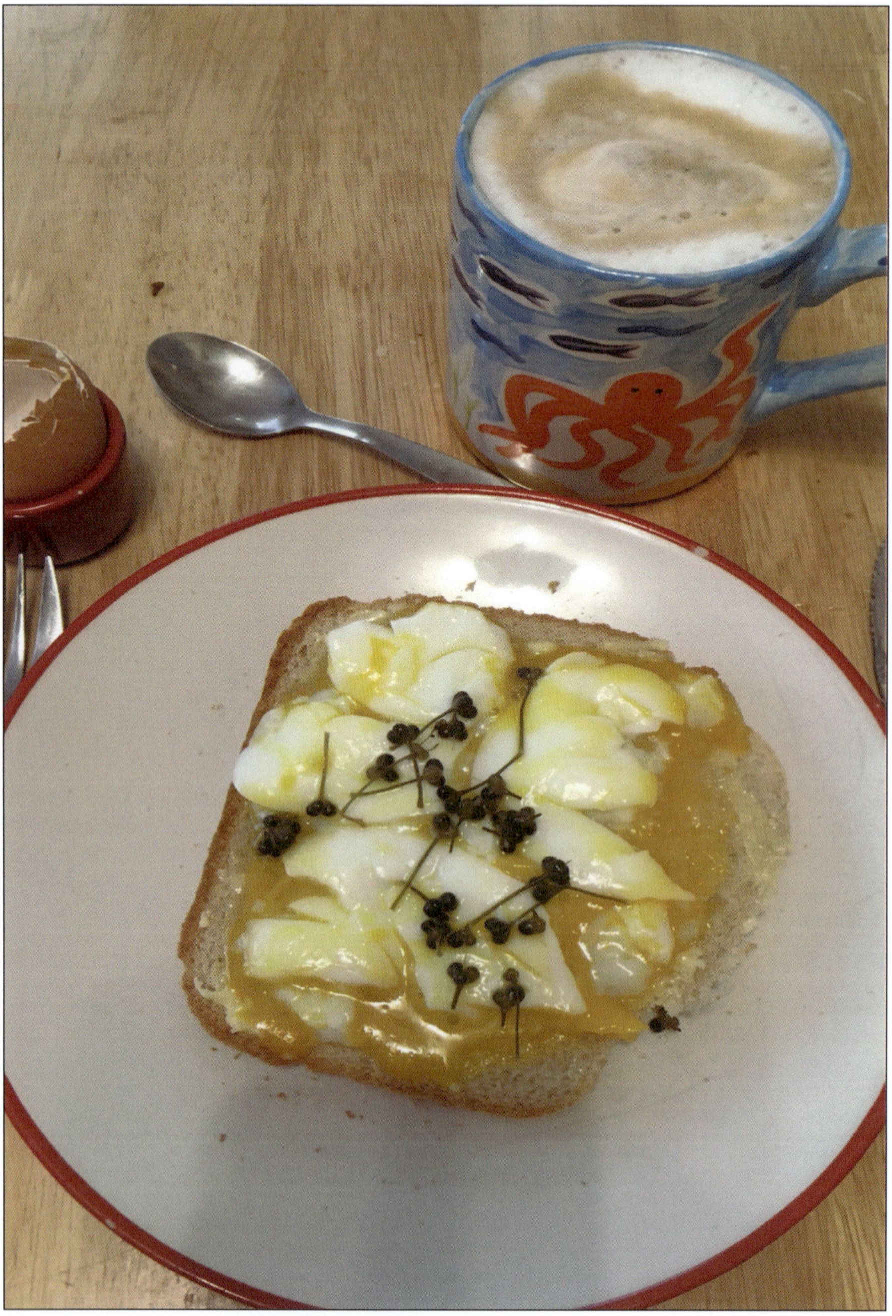

Condiments

Wild Garlic Oil

Prep Time: 5 mins

INGREDIENTS

500ml good quality olive oil (or any oil you like)
½ handful or 15g wild garlic

METHOD

1. Decant a small amount of the oil to make space for the wild garlic.
2. Gently crush the garlic leaves to release the flavour.
3. Push the leaves into the oil bottle ensuring that none of them poke above the oil.
4. Allow to infuse for a day or so before using.
5. As long as the leaves remain under the oil, the wild garlic oil will last as long as the oil does.
6. You can remove the leaves after a few days if you prefer, although I like a stronger intensity.

IDEAS FOR USE

- Pour into a small bowl and add some flakes of sea salt. Dunk pieces of chunky bread into the oil and salt. For added yum add a dollop of balsamic vinegar.
- Drizzle over pizza.
- Drizzle over risotto just before serving.
- Use in a salad dressing (4 parts oil to 1 part vinegar).
- Drizzle over steamed veg like broccoli, green beans or carrots.

Wild Garlic Butter

Prep Time: 5 mins

INGREDIENTS

¼ handful or 8g wild garlic (maybe about 8 leaves)
50-100g butter

METHOD

1. Finely chop the wild garlic either by hand or with a mini blender.
2. Mix into room-termpature butter. If it cold outside then blast the butter in a microwave for 5 seconds at a time to soften just enough (but try not to melt it).
3. Store in a jam jar in a fridge as you would butter

IDEAS FOR USE

- On jacket potatoes, instead of butter
- Stirred into risotto before serving.
- Use a large knob when steaming or baking fish.
- Dunk freshly baked doughballs in it instead of normal garlic butter.
- Slathered onto toast!
- Melted over freshly steamed veg.

Wild Garlic Mayonnaise

Prep Time: 5 mins

Works as a delicioous condiment where mayo is in order such as salad, egg mayonnaise sandwiches, and great for dipping breaded fish goujons in!

INGREDIENTS

½ handful or 15g wild garlic
100g good quality mayonnaise

METHOD

1. Finely chop the wild garlic either by hand or with a mini blender.
2. Mix into Mayonnaise.
3. Store in a jam jar in a fridge as you would mayo.

. IDEAS FOR USE

- Use to liven up a sandwich
- Instead of salad dressing.
- Dunk slices of pizza into it.
- Create an amazing potato salad with it.

Wild Garlic Vinegar

Prep Time: 5 mins

Not for the faint-hearted this powerful vinegar packs a punch and will make a fiery salad dressing, or give your chips some zing!

INGREDIENTS

¼ handful or 8g wild garlic

250ml vinegar either apple cider vinegar to enjoy additional health benefits, or something fairly gentle like white wine vinegar to allow the flavours to come through.

METHOD

1. Decant some of the vinegar to make space for the wild garlic leaves.
2. Stuff the leaves into the vinegar making sure all leaves are under the liquid.
3. Infuse for several days.
4. Use within a few months and ensure the leaves stay underneath the liquid or they tend to go mouldy.

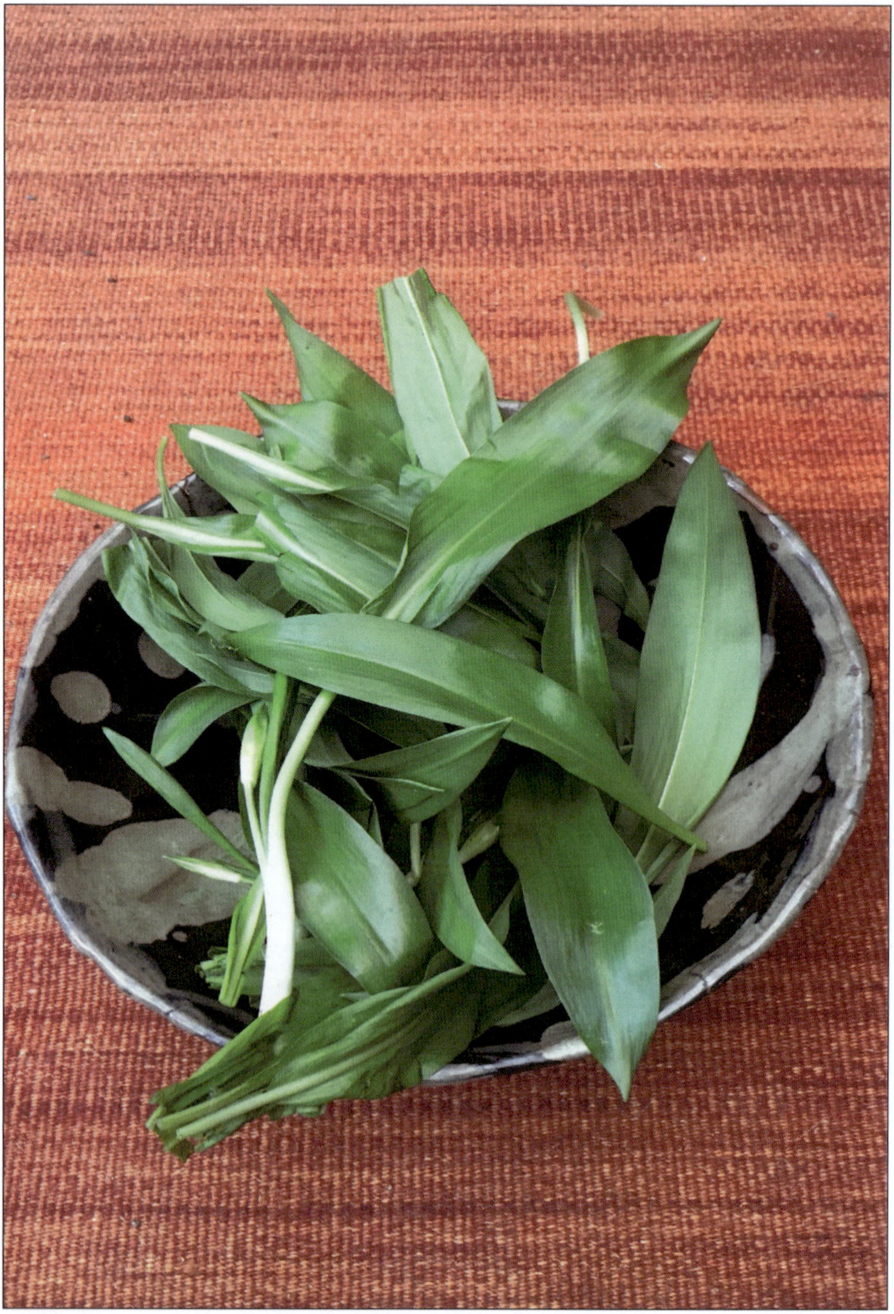

Wild Garlic Garnish

Prep time: 1 min

In a hurry or just want to enjoy the remains of your catch, this is probably the simplest way to enjoy wild garlic.

METHOD

1. Take 5-10 wild garlic leaves and chop as finely as required.
2. Liberally sprinkle on top of whatever you are eating!

Pickled Wild Garlic Flower Heads & Seed Pods

This is the simplest thing to do but does require quite a lot of flower heads or seed pods. Note you won't be able to do this at the same time but the recipe for each is the same.

The flower heads should be gathered before they have erupted from their mebrane when they look like little buds up to 2cm in lenth.

The seed pods are the little green balls left after the plant has flowered and the petals fall to reveal these little green diamonds of flavour. They have a three-part head and look like tiny alien heads!

Prep Time: 10 mins

Gather the buds/pods by pulling the flower heads off the plants.

INGREDIENTS

A bag full of wild garlic flower buds/seed pod heads (it's amazing how little you get from this!)

50ml vinegar either apple cider vinegar to enjoy additional health benefits, or something fairly gentle like white wine vinegar to allow the flavours to come through.

A teaspoon of mustard seeds

A few springs of dill (optional)

METHOD

1. Pluck all the buds/pods off the flower heads. You don't really want any of the stalk just the little pods.
2. If you think they got dirty you might wish to just wash them off. Best to let them dry before pickling.
3. Place in a clean (ideally sterilised jam jar – run through the dishwasher is fine).
4. Fill up the jar with vinegar and any other ingredients for flavour (mustard seeds and dill). The pods will rise to the top so good to keep the jar as full as pods as you can.
5. Leave for at least 48 hours.
6. Will last in the cupboard unopened until next year. Even opened they seem to last ages, although some might suggest putting them in the fridge. Ours always get eaten too quickly!

Wild Garlic Salad Dressing Vinaigrette

Salad dressing will vary hugely depending on the type of oil used, the strength of the vinegar and your personal preference. Something like apple cider vinegar will give a great flavour (and really good for you to boot) but may well smother the flavour of the oil.

Of course, using wild garlic vinegar will give you a double whammy!

This will be a bit trial and error and always follow the best cooks' rule: taste it, taste it, taste it.

Prep Time: 5 mins

INGREDIENTS

3 parts olive oil – Use the best quality extra virgin you can find for salad.

1 part vinegar – white wine vinegar is a good starting apple ider vinegar, you may want to reduce the amount to begin. You can also use lemon juice.

Small dollop of mustard (this acts as an emulsifier and will make it all cbind together and not separate so quickly).

A few handfuls of wild garlic (appropriate to the amount of dressing you are making).

Salt & pepper

METHOD

1. Easiest thing to do is chuck it all in the blender for a minute.

2. If you are cautious about the vinegar then add half the vinegar, blend, taste, then add some more, belnd, taste, until you feel you have got it right.

3. If you don't have a blender you can put it in a glass jar, screw the lid on tight and give it a really good shake. Obviously you'll have to chop the wild garlic very finely.

4. Slather over your chosen salad, or use Wild Garlic Bread to soak it up.

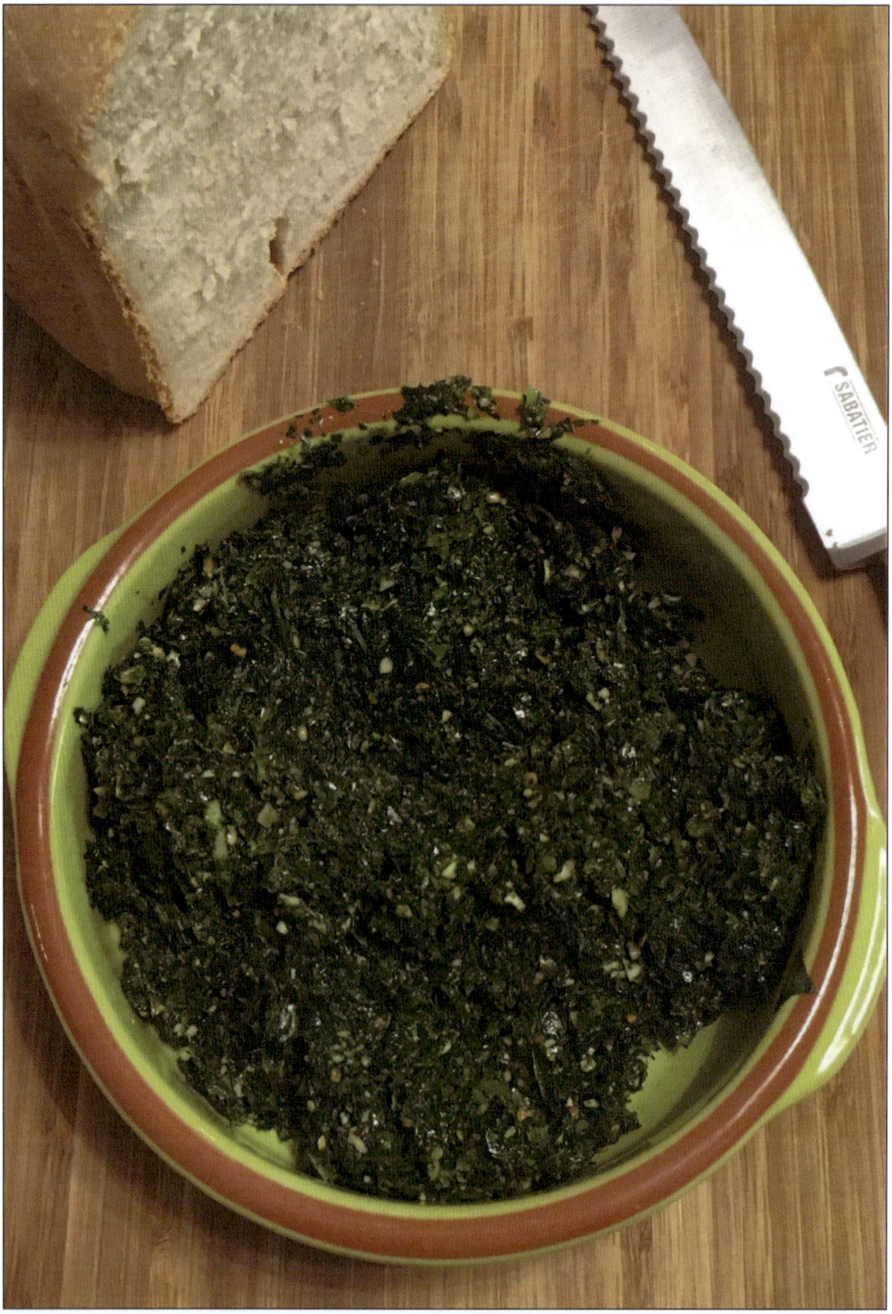
SABATIER

Sauces

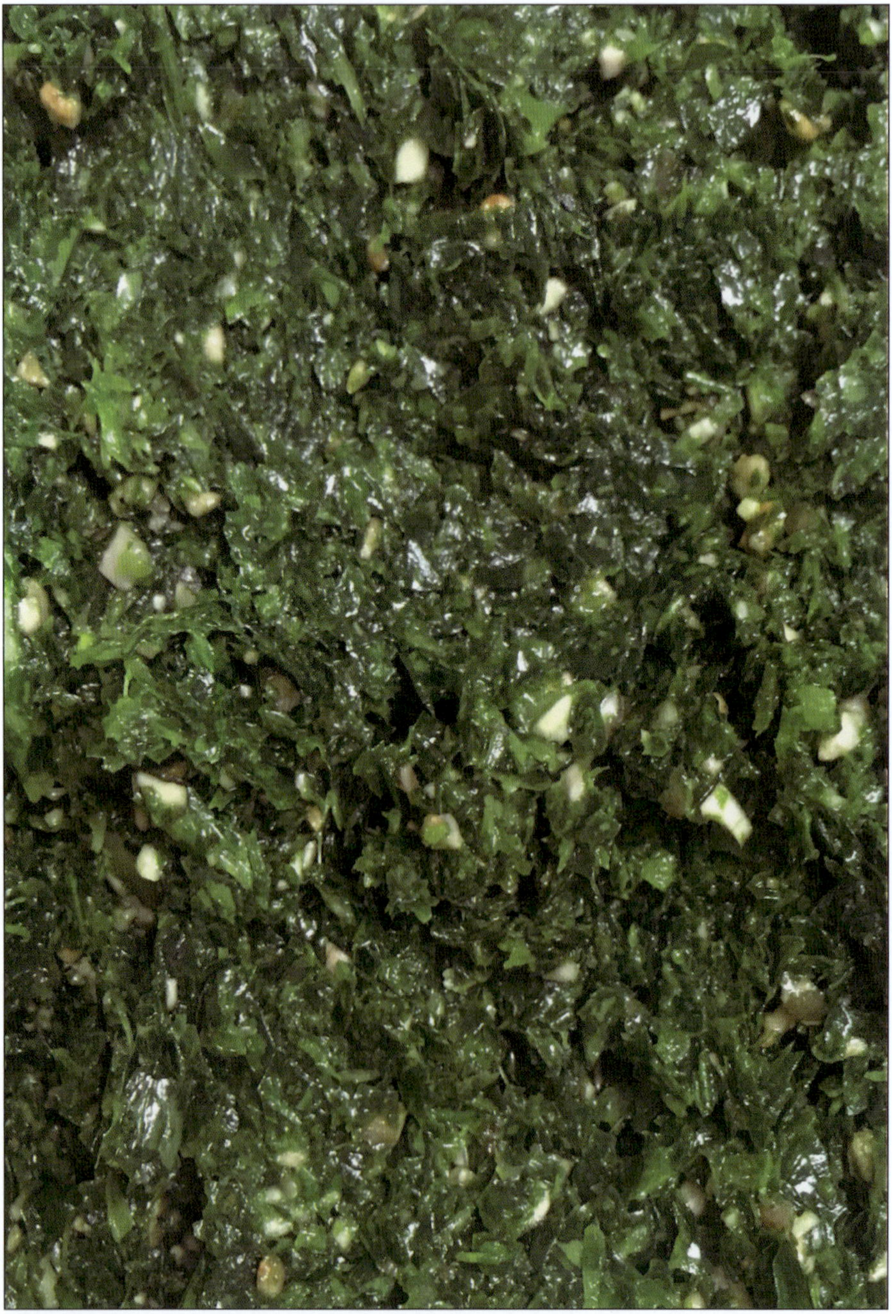

Wild Garlic Pesto

Prep Time: 10 mins

This cheeky little number can transform the dullest meal into a lip-smacking feast. Don't get hung up on quantities just have fun with it.

INGREDIENTS

4 handfuls or 120g wild garlic

1 handful or 30g of nuts or seeds (pine, almonds, pumpkin seeds, anything will do. I like hazelnuts best) lightly toasted

Optional 30g parmesan or parmigiana grated

A good few glugs or 50ml of extra virgin olive oil or your favourite oil

Salt to taste

METHOD

1. Set the oven to a low heat and roast the nuts until starting to smell delicious – maybe around 10 mins? Alternatively toast in a dry frying pan until you can smell the nuttiness or they start to pop.
2. Blitz the nuts in a blender
3. Add a few glugs of olive oil and then add as much wild garlic as you can fit in the blender, adding the rest as the batches mulch down.
4. Blitz in short burts making sure to frequently clear the sides of the blender to ensure an even blitz.
5. Add the parmesan and blitz to blend it all in.
6. Add oil and a pinch or so of salt as required to get a consistency of pesto. Keep blitzing and tasting until you are happy.
7. Store in a jam jar in a fridge and eat within a week. It is a good idea to ensure there is a top layer of oil and this helps to preserve the pesto.

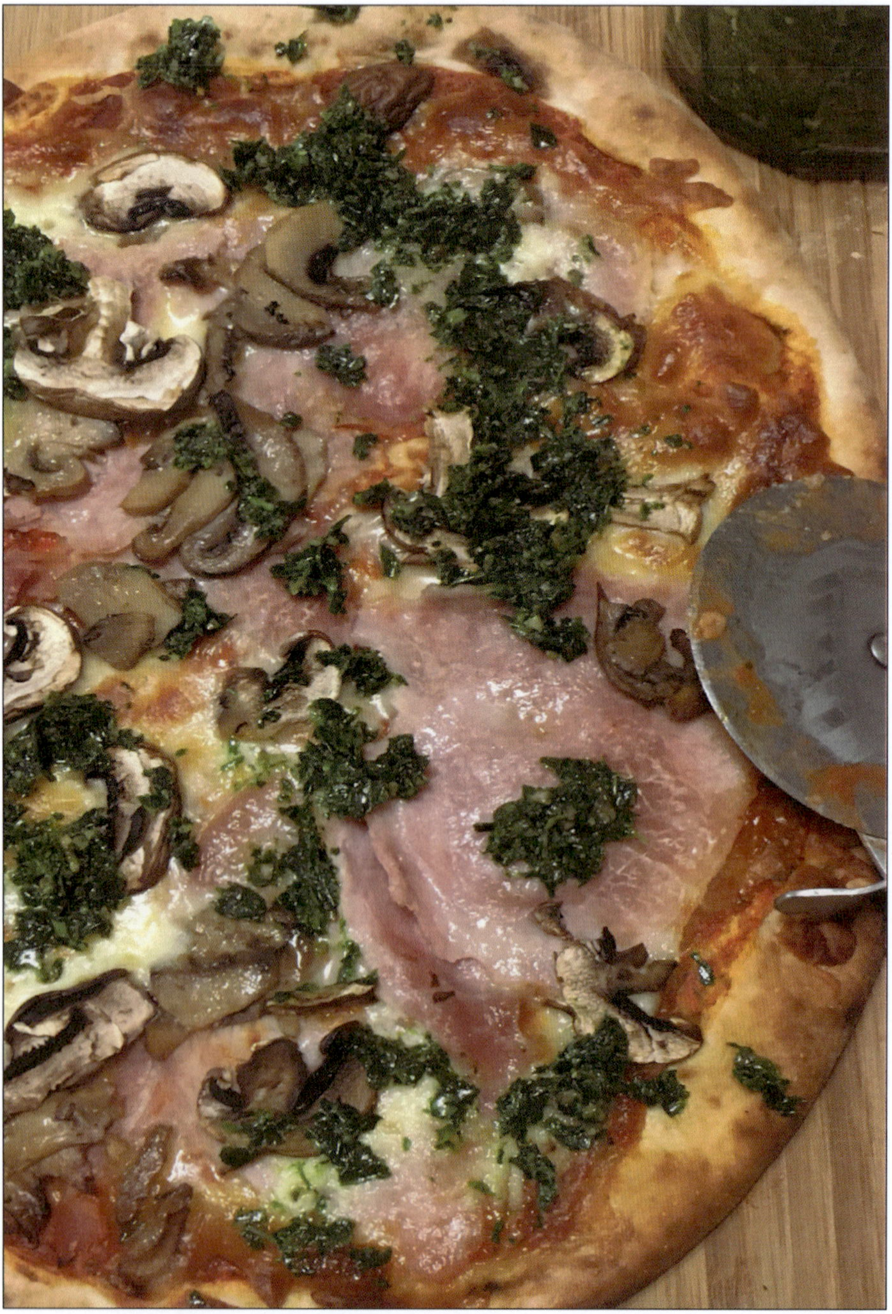

IDEAS FOR USE

Wild garlic pesto is my favourite thing to do with it and used liberally with every meal like a condiment.

You can store it in the freezer successfully as well in a plastic container. Hummus or cottage cheese pots work really well (make sure you sellotape the lid to the pot).

1. Spaghetti with wild garlic pesto.
2. Use to liven up a cheese & ham sandwich.
3. Add a dollop to a hearty soup.
4. Add a dollop to liven up cottage cheese, hummus or any boring dip.
5. Eat with cheese and crackers.
6. On toast with a fried egg.
7. On top of a jacket potato with lashings of butter and yoghurt.
8. Mix into basmati rice to make a pseto rice, and serve with poached salmon.
9. Mix a dollop into a risotto to give it a kick.
10. Slather it over a chicken breast and gently roast it.
11. Add to any pizza or use it instead of tomatoe sauce if you want a pizza with a kick.

Wild Garlic Salsa

Prep Time: 10 mins (this salsa is best prepared an hour or few before eating to allow the flavours to mix together)

Using wild garlic in salsa adds a unique dimension to this scrumtious latin american sauce. Salsa just means "sauce" in Spanish but I use it more like a condiment with corn tortilla chips as my spoon.

While you could do this in a blender it really won't do it any justice and you'll probably end up with a salsa ketchup! Roughly chop to give it texture as well as flavour.

The real trick with salsa is to not allow the onion to overpower it so always start with the tomatoes and add the other ingredients mixing and tasting all the time to ensure you get the right balance.

INGREDIENTS

1 handful or 30 g wild garlic

200g good quality tomatoes, I prefer to use cherry tomatoes, finely chopped and keep the juice

½ small red or white onion finely chopped

Juice of 1 lime or lemon

1 chilli (or as much as you dare!), very finely chopped

Optional ½ handful or 15g fresh coriander, finely chopped

A glug or two of olive oil

Salt to taste

METHOD

1. Finely chop the tomatoes and add to a big bowl.
2. Finely chop the wild garlic and add all of it.
3. Finely chop the onion and add half, mix, then add more as you see fit. I think the ratio of tomato to onion should be around 2:1 but this is very much personal taste.
4. Add the lime juice, chilli, coriander if using, a generous pinch of salt and mix thoroughly. Taste.
5. Add olive oil if you feel it needs liquid and any other ingredient as required. Keep tasting and mixing until you feel you have got the right blend.
6. Leave to mung together for at least an hour and taste again befor serving.

Works brilliantly with corn tortilla chips, tacos, and to accompany huevos rancheros or any mexican dish.

Wild Garlic Salsa Verde

Prep Time: 10 mins

A green version of a salsa, this one more like a herby mix than a chilli tomato one. Again, chop and mix by hand for best results. This salsa works really well with strong fishy and meaty flavours like salmon or steak.

INGREDIENTS

1 handful or 30g wild garlic
1 handful or 30g parsley
1 handful or 30g basil
1 handful or 30g mint
1 tablespoon capers

5 anchovy filets
3-4 small gherkins
A few glugs of nice vinegar
30ml extra virgin olive oil
Salt to taste

METHOD

1. Finely chop all the leaves, capers and gherkins and mix in a large bowl.
2. Mash up the anchovy filets in a bit of olive oil to encourage them to disintegrate.
3. Add the anchovy, vinegar, olive oil and a pinch of salt to the mixture and combine well.
4. Taste and adjust the vinegar/oil ratio if need be. You won't need to salt this so much due to the anchovies so watch out when seasoning.
5. Store in a jam jar in the fridge.

Wild Garlic Guacamole

Prep Time: 5 mins

We never want to overpower guacamole with strong flavours and again you'll need lots of tasting to ensure you get a good balance.

INGREDIENTS

¼ handful or 8g wild garlic
2 ripe avocados
1 small chilli (to taste)
Juice of half or quarter of a lime or lemon
3 cherry tomatoes finely chopped (optional)
A few glugs of extra virgin olive oil
Salt to taste

METHOD

1. Finely chop the wild garlic either by hand or with a mini blender.
2. Scoop out the avocado ointo a bowl and mash up with a fork.
3. Chop the cherry tomatoes and mix with the avocado and wild garlic.
4. Add half the lime juice, olive oil, chilli and a pinch of salt. Mix it all up and taste.
5. Adjust lime juice , oil, chilli and salt to get the right balance.

A perfect complement to wild garlic salsa and lashings of nachos.

Wild Garlic Hummus

Prep Time: 5 mins

How strong you want your hummus will depend on your taste so use a little at a time and keep tasting it to get the right balance for you.

The consistency of the chickpeas and the amount of wild garlic will all affect the texture and you ned to experiment somewhat to get the right balance.

INGREDIENTS

¼ handful or 8g wild garlic
1 tin chickpeas
Approx. 30ml extra virgin olive oil (you may need more or less)
Salt to taste

METHOD

1. Rinse off the chickpeas and put into a blender (a Nutribullet also works).
2. Add half the wild garlic, and half the oil and blend for a minute or so.
3. Check the consistency and add more oil if the chickpeas are not really blending together.
4. Add salt and more oil and wild garlic a bit at a time and keep tasting it to check.
5. You usually need to add more oil than you expect.

Serve with toasted pitta bread or sticks of carrot, cucumber and celery.

Wild Garlic Dip

Prep Time: 5 mins

This makes a smoother and more creamy version of Wild Garlic Pesto and can be used in a similar fashion.

INGREDIENTS

1 handful or 30g wild garlic
1 tub cream cheese/soft cheese/ricotta
Salt to taste

METHOD

1. Put all ingredients into a blender and whizz until it has a fine consistency.
2. Taste it and mix it up and add more salt/wild garlic if required.

Serve on crackers with smoked salmon.

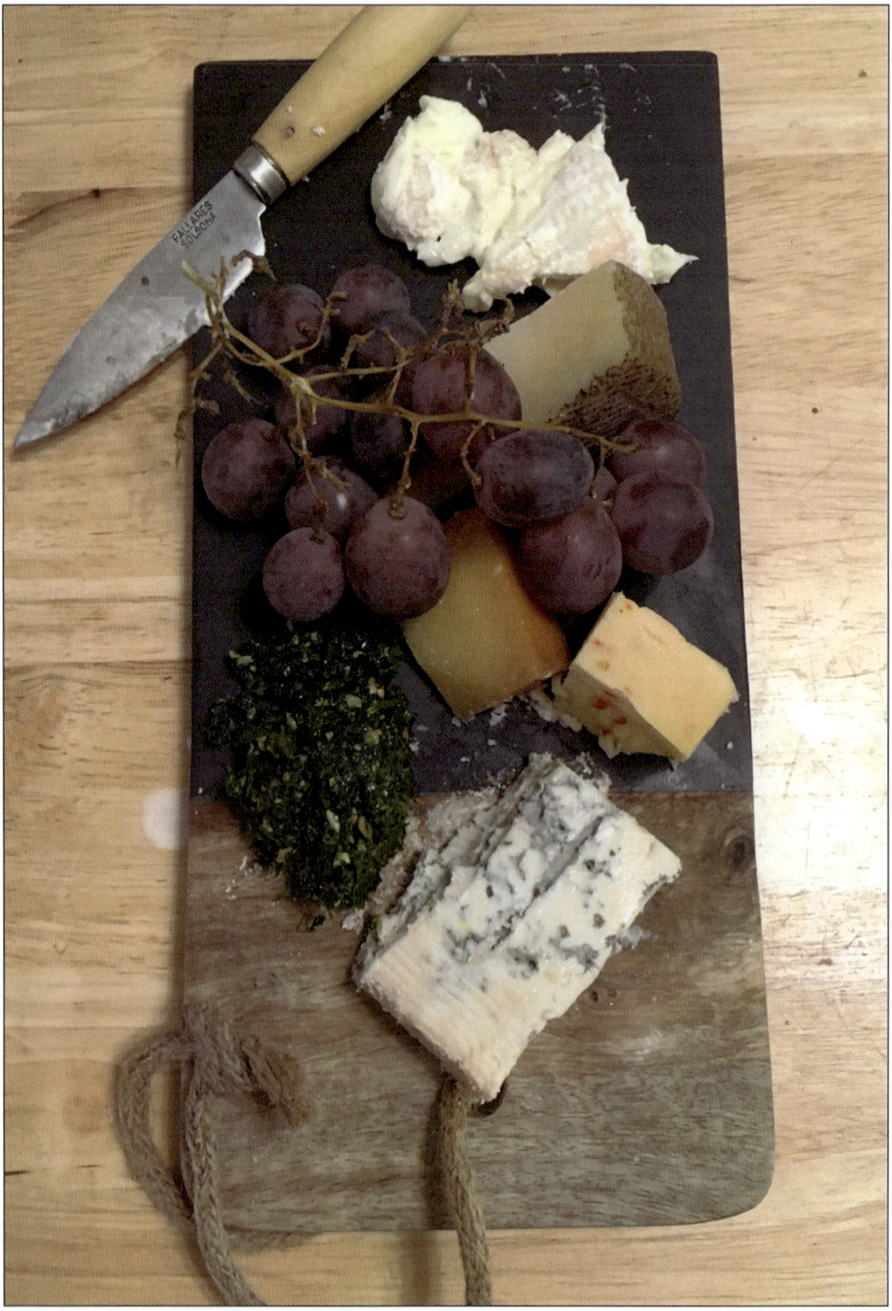
PALLARES
SOLSONA

Cold Dishes

Wild Garlic Bread

This is a take on your standard baguette garlic bread.

Prep time: 5-10 mins

INGREDIENTS

100g wild garlic butter or just plain butter
2 tablespoons wild garlic pesto
1 par-baked baguette or a baguette around 30cm long

METHOD

1. Turn on oven to temperature as directed on the baguette packet, or around Gas mark 4 or 180 degrees.
2. Mix the wild garlic pesto and butter together.
3. Slice the baguette diagonally not quite cutting all the way through, making each piece about 2cm thick.
4. Spread the wild garlic butter/pesto combo into each slit. You need at least a teaspoonful for each slit.
5. Wrap in tin foil and place in the oven. There is a way to wrap it where you place it in the middle of the foil and bring the top and borttom to meet. Now take each ends and roll them in to the ends of the baguette. Now roll down the top making a sort-of pouch. You can easily unroll it to check if it is melted/cooked.
6. Cook for directed time or around 10 minutes until the butter is all melted.
7. Serve with wild garlic risotto.

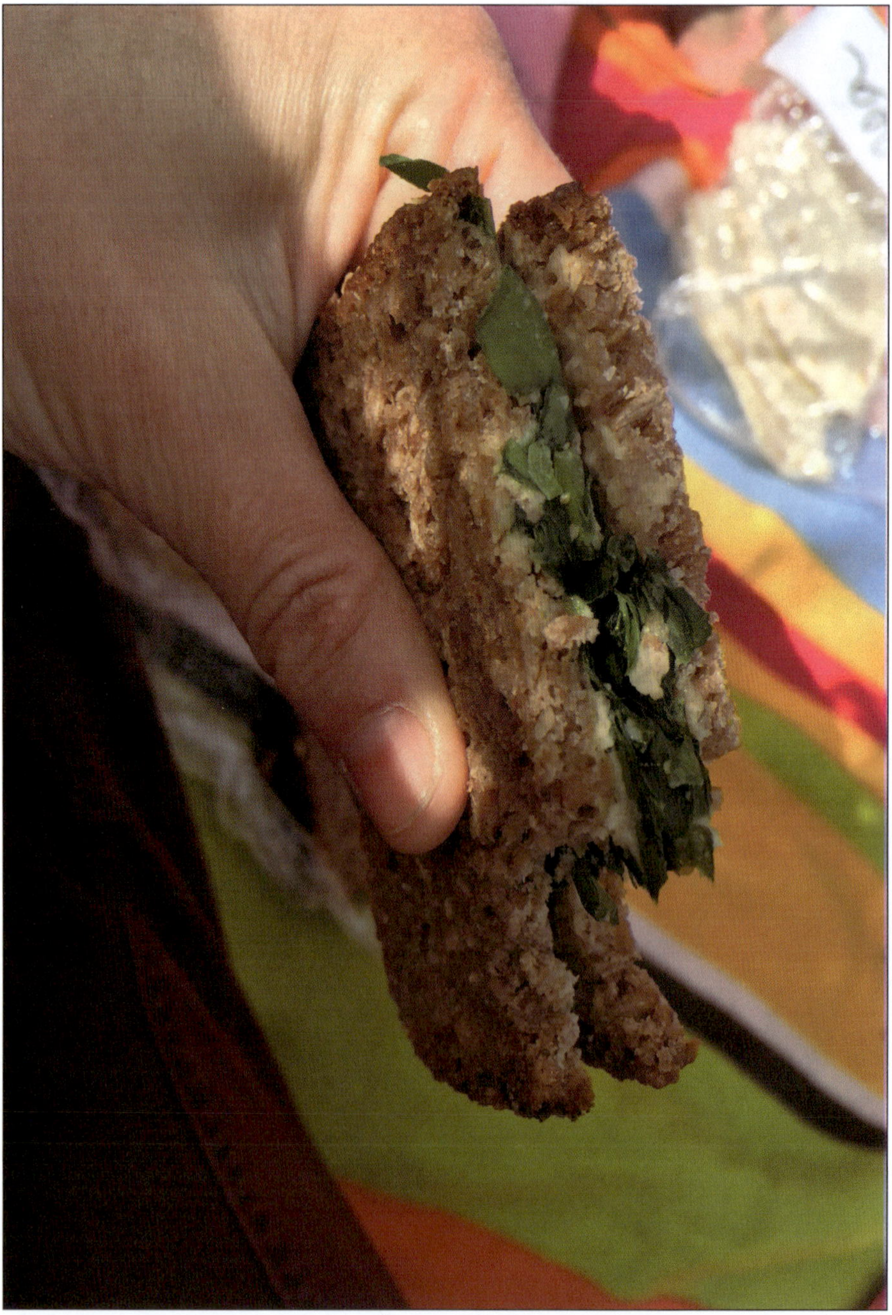

Wild Garlic & Egg Mayo Sandwiches

Prep Time: 15 mins

Egg mayo sandwiches are truly scrumptious but need hard-boiled cold eggs. You can pre-boil the eggs and keep in the shells in the fridge for up to a week. If you are short of time you could just use scrambled eggs. I won't tell.

INGREDIENTS

1 egg
2 slices bread
¼ handful or 8g wild garlic chopped
1 tablespoon good quality mayonnaise

METHOD

1. Put the egg in a pan of water and bring to the boil, and simmer for around 10 minutes.
2. Place the egg into cold water for 5 minutes or so to cool down. You can use warm eggs but it tends to make the mayo go a bit funny.
3. Peel the eggs, chop in a bowl and add the mayo and chopped wild garlic. Mix well. Add salt to taste.
4. Slather between your bread.

Other Sandwich Ideas

Wild garlic's amazing flavour is best enjoyed raw and makes a fabulous addition to a number of sandwiches.

Liberal amounts of wild garlic pesto also make any sandwich the Queen of Sandwiches.

Ham, cheese & wild garlic sandwich (use either fresh wild garlic leaves or wild garlic pesto).

Smoked salmon, cream cheese & wild garlic pesto bagel.

Wild garlic hummus and cucumber sandwich.

Wild garlic, cheese, lettuce and tomato wrap (use fresh leaves or pesto).

Wild Garlic Devilled Eggs

Prep Time: 15 mins

Again hard-boiled eggs are required for this. It is a bit of a retro dish and usually served at a party rather than as a meal but I was inspired a by a pesto version and thought it would be perfect with wild garlic.

INGREDIENTS

2 eggs
1 tablespoon wild garlic pesto or wild garlic mayo
A few leaves for garnish

METHOD

1. Boil the eggs for 10 minutes to hard boil.
2. Place the eggs in cold water for 5 mins.
3. Carefully peel the eggs and slice lengthways.
4. Scoop out the yolks into a bowl and squish them with a fork, add the wild garlic pesto.
5. Mix really well then spoon the mixture back into the egg halves. (If you are really fancy you could use an icing piper bag to make pretty patterns!)
6. Serve with a garnish of finely chopped wild garlic.

Potato Salad with Wild Garlic

Prep Time: 20 mins

This variation on potato salad is a fab in a summer picnic lunch.

INGREDIENTS

300g new or waxy potatoes
2 eggs (hardboiled)
A few dollops of wild garlic mayonnaise
A handful of capers
Extra handful of wild garlic, torn
Salt & Pepper to taste

METHOD

1. Chop the potatoes into small pieces. I prefer then to be around 2-3 cm but you can make them smaller if preferred.
2. Place the potatoes in a steamer or pan of boiling water and add the eggs in their shells.
3. Steam or boil until tender. Usually 10-15 mins if cut up but check regularly with a sharp knife to ensure they don't get overcooked or they will just fall apart.
4. Drain when cook and allow the potatoes & eggs to completely cool. You can soak in cold water if you want to speed this process up.
5. Peel the eggs and chop roughly.
6. Place the potatoes, eggs, capers in a bowl and add enough wild garlic mayonnaise to cover the potatoes and egg.
7. Season well with salt and pepper & garnish with wild garlic.

Wild Garlic Light Salad

Prep Time: 5 mins

Is it really necessary to create a recipe for salad? Probably not but sometimes it is nice to give you inspiration.

INGREDIENTS

A couple of handfuls of wild garlic, torn up
A handful of rocket
Half a Romano or little gem lettuce, chopped
5-10 cherry tomatoes, halved
A few inches of cucumber, sliced
Pickled wild garlic seed pods
Good quality olive Oil
Sea salt

METHOD

1. Chop everything up and mix together in a bowl.
2. Drizzle with olive oil.
3. Add salt to taste.

Wild Garlic Heavy Salad

Prep Time: 10 mins

Sometimes you want a cold spring salad but need a bit more sustenance. Again, the ingredients listed are more for inspiration than anything else. It's a great way to use up leftovers. This recipe is a bit like a wild garlic nicoise.

INGREDIENTS

Handfuls of wild garlic, torn
Romano or little gem lettuce, chopped
Cherry tomatoes, halved
Boiled new potatoes (cold), halved or quartered depending on size
Hard boiled eggs, quartered lengthways
French green beans (steamed for 5 mins max)
Artichoke hearts (tinned is easiest)
Black olives (or green if you prefer)
Capers or pickled wild garlic pods
Fresh Tuna/Salmon (please don't use tinned fish – it's a travesty) lightly steamed.

METHOD

Chuck it all into a bowl and liberally apply wild garlic salad dressing.

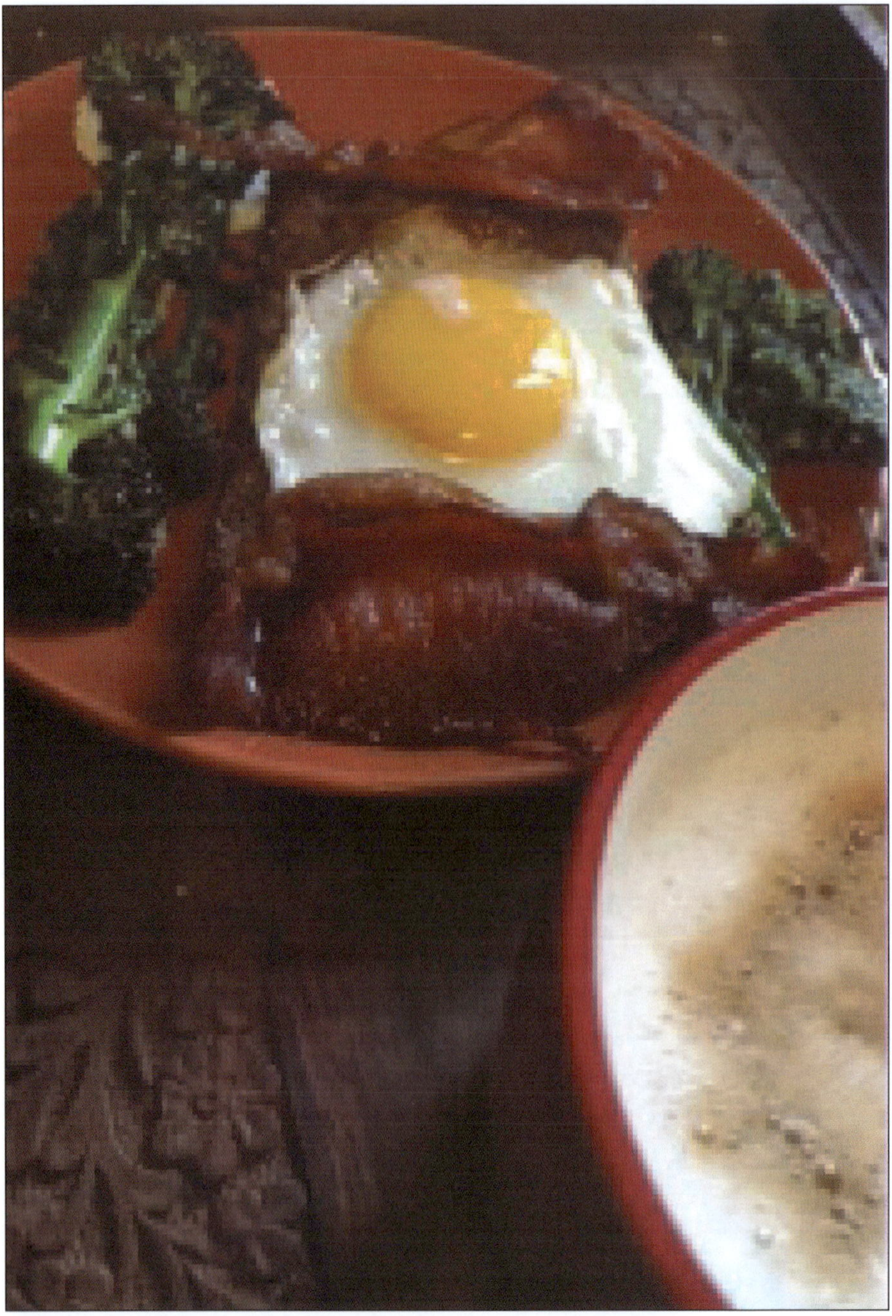

Hot Dishes

Wild Garlic & Mushroom Pancakes

Prep Time: 20 mins

Pancakes are such wonderfully simple staples but can be the basis for any number of delicious fillings. Here are a few ideas of how to bring savoury pancakes to the table. Especially as pancake day falls bang in the middle of wild garlic season.

INGREDIENTS - FOR PANCAKES

Makes about 6 large pancakes

1 mug or 140g plain flour
1 large egg
1 mug or 250ml milk
Butter or olive oil

FOR FILLING

15g butter
1 small onion, finely chopped.
100g mushrooms roughly chopped
1 handful or 30g wild garlic

METHOD

FOR THE PANCAKES

1. Blend the pancake ingredients altogether untill well mixed.
2. Allow pancake mixture to settle for 20-30 minutes at room temperature (optional).
3. In a clean frying pan on a moderate to high heat add a glug of olive oil or butter.
4. Pour half a ladle of pancake mixture into the pan and swirl the pan to cover the bottom. You ideally want to have about 2mm depth of mixture.
5. Allow the mixture to cook on one side for a few minutes, then flip and cook the other side.
6. When cooked add to a plate and cook all the rest of the pancake mixture. To reheat the pancakes pop them in the microwave for a minute or so.

FOR THE FILLING

1. Melt the butter in a frying pan and add the finely chopped onion. Fry on a low heat for 10 minutes or onions are going translucent.
2. Add the mushrooms, possibly adding some extra butter or olive oil if the pan seems dry. Saute with the onions for another 10 minutes or so.
3. Mix the chopped wild garlic through the hot mixture and leave in pan to wilt as you make the pancakes.
4. To serve dollop the mixture into a pancake and roll up.

Wild Garlic & Blue Cheese Pancakes

Prep Time: 10 mins

See mushroom pancake recipe.

INGREDIENTS

1 handful or 30g wild garlic
50g blue cheese

METHOD

Crumble blue cheese and wild garlic leaves onto a pancake and roll to eat.

Wild Garlic Soup

Prep Time: 20 mins

When you cook wild garlic you start to lose some of the intense flavour but you can still come up with delicious ways to include it in a meal.

INGREDIENTS

1 small onion, finely chopped
A few glugs of olive oil
1 large or 2 small potatoes, peeled and finely chopped
1 litre hot stock
Salt & pepper to taste
3 handfuls or 90g wild garlic, roughly chopped
One glug of wild garlic oil

METHOD

1. Heat the olive oil in a saucepan and add the chopped onion.
2. Saute for 5 mins on a low to medium heat.
3. Add the potatoes and allow to saute for a couple of minutes.
4. Add the stock, bring to the boil and simmer until potatoes soften.
5. Add the wild garlic and bring back to a simmer, add seasoning as required.
6. Serve chunky or put through a blender to have a smooth soup.
7. Add a dollop of wild garlic oil to serve to enhance the wild garlic flavour.
8. Serve with chunky farmhouse bread with lashings of butter or toasted pitta bread.

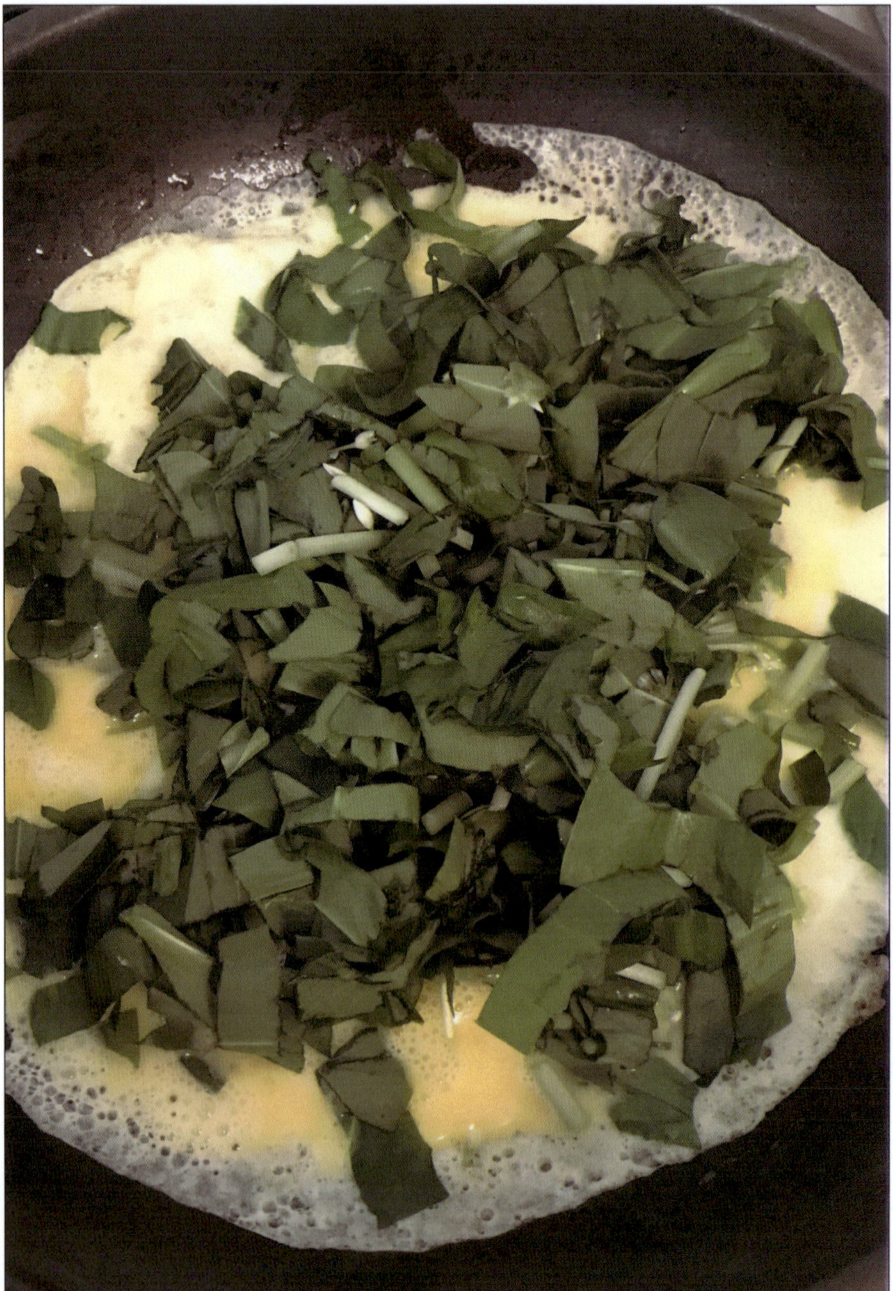

Wild Garlic Omelette

Prep Time: 10 mins

This omelette recipe uses wild garlic in the actual egg mixture, although you could make a plain omelette and then fold over fresh wild garlic leaves (see picture). Or maybe use any of the pancake fillings. Or both! Remember omelettes should be cooked hot and quickly.

INGREDIENTS

1 handful or 30 g wild garlic
2-3 eggs

METHOD

1. Chop the wild garlic fairly fine.
2. Whisk the eggs until light and fluffy.
3. Mix in the wild garlic.
4. Heat a large pan with a few glugs of olive oil.
5. When hot add the omelette mix and cook on a high heat.
6. If need be move the mixture around a little bit to allow the liquid eggs to touch the surface of the pan.
7. Fold in half and serve with salad leaves.

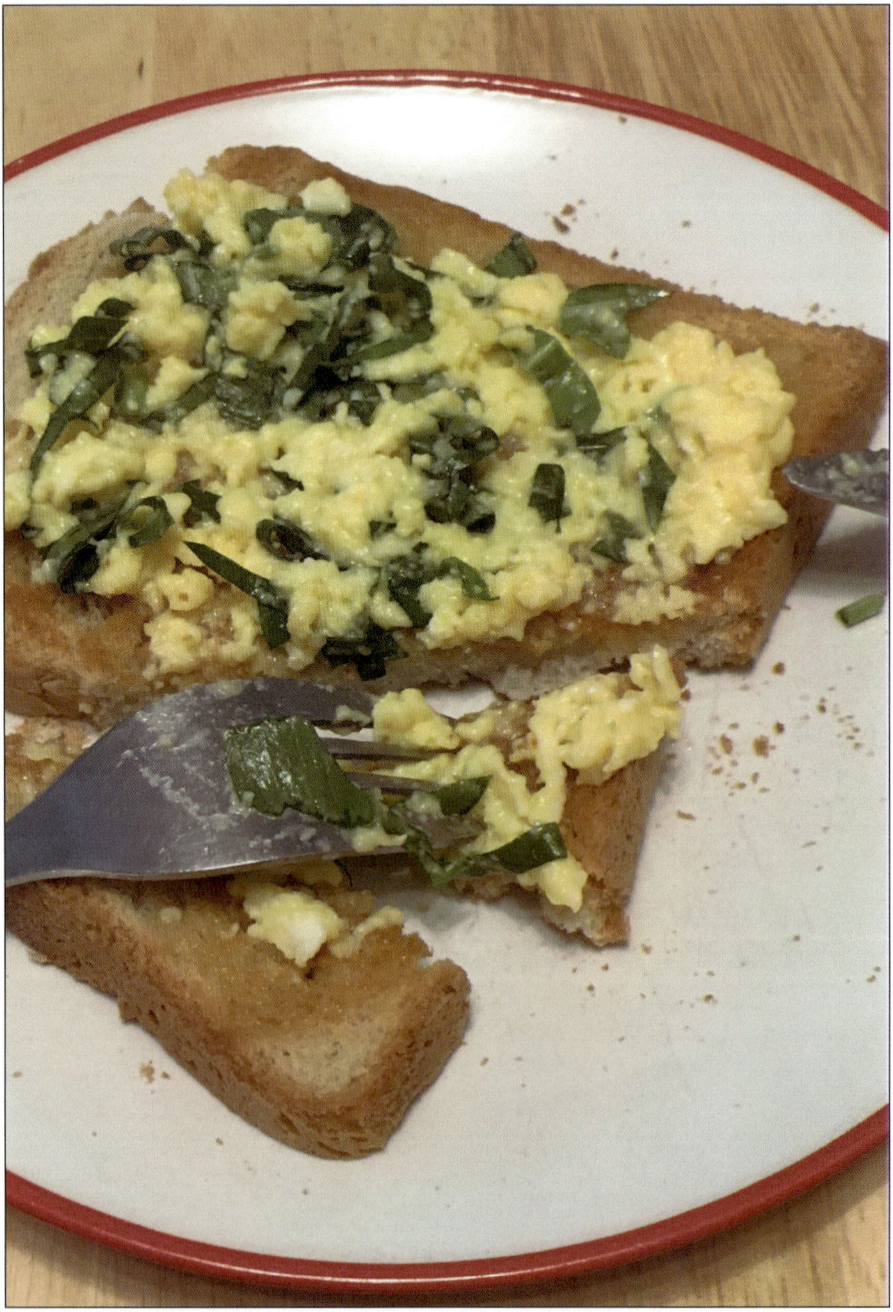

Wild Garlic Scrambled Egg

Prep Time: 10 mins

Wild garlic and eggs are a match made in heaven. You can just use wild garlic to garnish any egg dish but I quite like to add it to the mixture. The best scrambled eggs are cooked slowly on a low heat.

INGREDIENTS

1 handful or 30 g wild garlic
2-3 eggs
Knob of butter

METHOD

1. Finely chop the wild garlic.
2. Whisk the eggs until light and fluffy.
3. Add a knob of butter to a non-stick saucepan and gentle melt on a low heat.
4. Add the eggs and stir frequently as they cook to scramble them.
5. When they are 90% cooked take off the heat and stir in the wild garlic.
6. Serve on toasted Sourdough bread, or my preference is a strong rye bread toast.

A coddler is a kind of ceramic egg cup with a metal lid with a loop. It acts like an egg boiler but without the shell and added yummy ingredients. The egg takes a few minutes longer to cook and is worth the trial and error to see how long it needs for your coddler. It is worth all the effort!

Wild Garlic Coddled Eggs with Cheese

Prep Time: 10 mins

INGREDIENTS

A glug of oil or butter
3 wild garlic leaves, sliced
A few slices of cheese
1 egg

METHOD

1. Smear the inside of the coddler with butter or oil including the lid (the egg sticks and is a bugger to wash up if you don't grease it).
2. Line the coddler with the cheese and the wild garlic leaves.
3. Carefully break the egg into the coddler.
4. Add a bit of cheese/leaf to the top.
5. Screw on the lid tight.
6. Boil a pan of water with enough water so that the coddler is just covered but the loop is sticking out of the water.
7. Gently lower the coddler into the pan (a wooden spoon handle through the loop works well).
8. Boil for around 5-6 minutes for a soft yolk, 10-12 for a hard one.
9. Carefully remove coddler from pan, unscrew lid and eat like a boiled egg.

Wild Garlic Heuvos Rancheros

Prep Time: 25 mins

This amazing mexican breakfast is really the breakfast of kings! It can be made with anything you have in your fridge so play around with the ingredients. My hubby likes to use blood sausage in his but bleurgh! These ingredients are a guide but the ones marked with * are probably non-negotiable. For a veggie version just omit the chorizo and replace with a glug of chilli oil. We like to chop the ingredients into big chunks but it is very much a matter of taste.

INGREDIENTS

1 large onion chopped*
1 chilli chopped*
2 sweet peppers chopped*
3 inches of chorizo, sliced (or a glut of chilli oil if you are veggie)
2 tomatoes or a few tablespoons of passata/pasta sauce
2 teaspoons smoked paprika*
A few tablespoons of cooked red kidney beans or black beans
2 handfuls or 60 g wild garlic*
1 egg per person*
1 tortilla per person (or toast)
1 handful or 30g fresh coriander, chopped
1 avocado
1 large handful of wild garlic

METHOD

1. Fry the onion, peppers, chorizo, and tomatoes until they start to soften.
2. Add the smoked paprika and the beans and stir well. Add a little bit of water if things look a bit dry.
3. Add the wild garlic and stir through and take pan off the heat.
4. In a fresh clean pan heat a glug of olive oil and fry the eggs to taste.
5. In the meantime heat the tortilla in the microwave or oven.
6. Lay the tortilla on a plate, add the mixture and lay the friend egg on top.
7. Garnish with fresh coriander, a few extra chopped leaves of wild garlic and salt and avocado on the side and perhaps servce with a dollop of wild garlic salsa, and some wild garlic guacamole.

Jacket Potato with Wilted Wild Garlic & Nutmeg

Prep Time: 5 minutes for filling, up to 60 mins for potato depending on size

INGREDIENTS

1 large potato
1 knob of butter
3 handfuls or 90 g wild garlic
Nutmeg to taste

METHOD

1. Heat the oven to Gas 6 or 180 degrees.
2. Pierce the potato skin in a number of places and bake in the oven until soft (check after 30 minutes to judge progress).
3. When potato is ready, heat the butter in a pan on a low heat and add the wild garlic.
4. Wilt for 1-2 minutes.
5. Remove from heat and grate nutmeg over the top.
6. Serve on jacket potato with a dollop of mayo.

An alternative to this recipe is using a big dollop of wild garlic pesto.

Rik's Wild Garlic & Fried Egg Sandwich

Prep Time: 10 mins

Our dear friend Rik is a fan of the friend egg sandwich PLUS! This recipe is in his honour!

INGREDIENTS

2 slices good chunky bread
5 sun dried tomatoes (or cherry tomatoes), chopped
½ an avocado, sliced
1 egg
½ handful or 15 g wild garlic

METHOD

1. Lightly toast the bread.
2. Layer up the sun-dried tomatoes, avocado and wild garlic leaves.
3. Fry the egg and layer on top.
4. Season with salt and pepper.
5. Add the top slice and dig in!

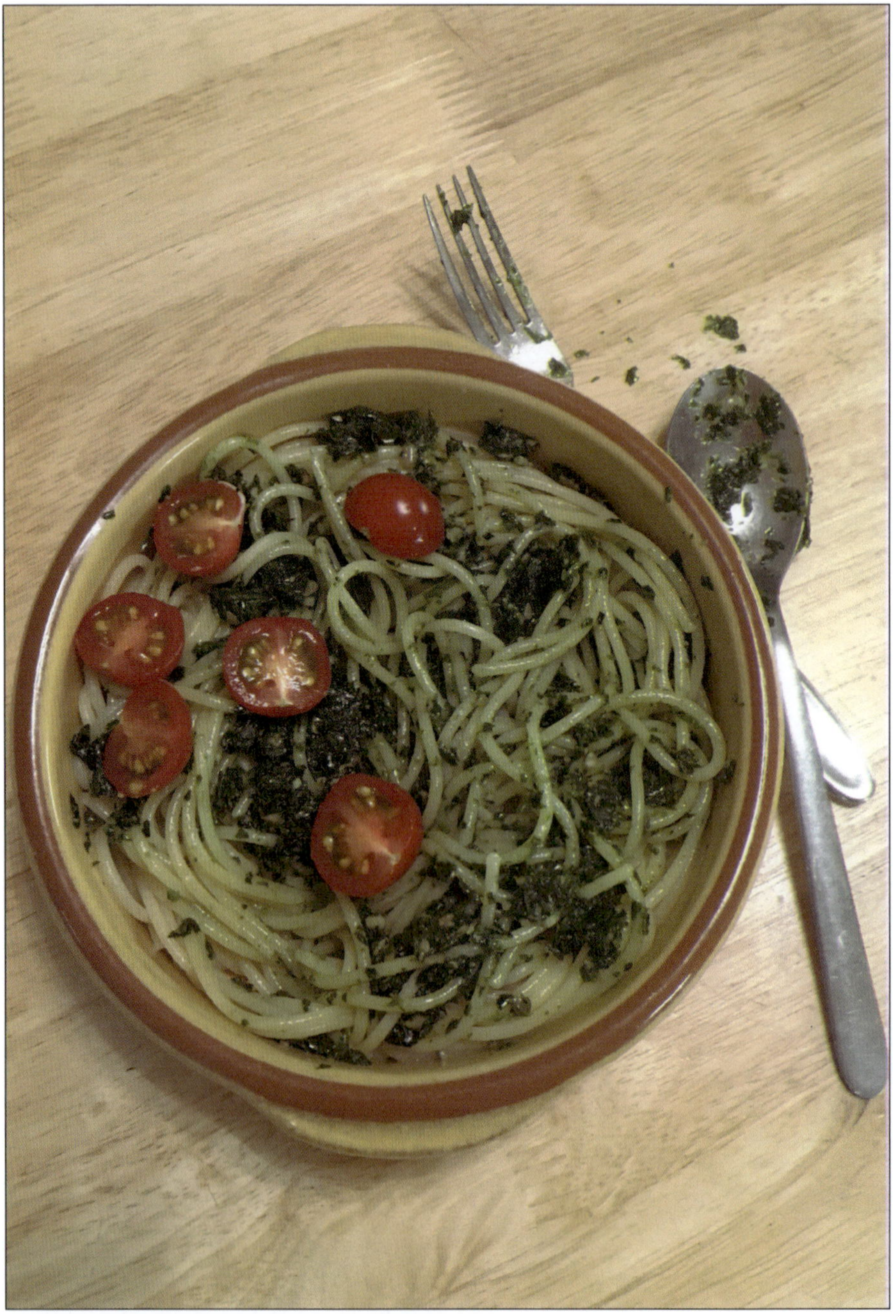

Spaghetti & Wild Garlic Pesto

Prep time: 10 mins

INGREDIENTS

80-100g spaghetti per person (in fact any pasta will do)
Large dollop of wild garlic pesto

METHOD

1. Bring a pan of water to the boil.
2. Add a blob of olive oil.
3. Bunch up the spaghetti and place it in the middle of the pan letting go so that all the pasta falls evenly apart.
4. With a wooden spoon gently pat the spaghetti ends until they bend and submerge.
5. Set the timer for 10 mins (or however long the instructions indicate).
6. Make sure you stir the pasta after a frew minutes to ensure it is not sticking.
7. Drain spaghetti and toss in wild garlic pasta.
8. Serve with tomato, mozzarella & wild garlic salad.

Baked Salmon with Wild Garlic Pesto Rice

Prep time: 20 mins

INGREDIENTS

75g basmati rice per person
Wild garlic pesto
1 salmon steak or fillet per person
A little olive oil
Salt & pepper

METHOD

1. Turn on oven to Gas Mark 5 or 200 degrees.
2. Measure out the rice and place in a pan that has a lid.
3. Rinse the rice until the water runs clear and tip the water out.
4. Add enough water so that there is twice as much volume of water than rice.
5. Bring to the boil with the lid on (takes a few minutes).
6. Check it is boiling then replace lid before switching off the heat.
7. DO NOT OPEN THE LID.
8. Leave for 15 mins (this makes perfect rice every time).
9. Now place the salmon in an ovenproof dish and rub with oil and season with salt & pepper.
10. Place in the oven for around 10 mins or until Salmon is done to

your taste. (Note, I prefer salmon only just cooked in the middle – leave it too long and it will be dry and a bit tough. You can eat salmon raw so don't be afraid to take it out when the middle is still darker pink.)

11. When the rice is done, add a few dollops of Wild Garlic Pesto and mix thoroughly.

12. Serve the rice with the baked salmon.

Wild Garlic Risotto

I love Jamie Oliver's recipe for risotto but it is a fairly generic recipe that is similar in most cases. The alcohol is optional (all the alcohol will burn off in cooking) but it does help to give it a lovely flavour.

Prep time: 30-40 mins

INGREDIENTS

A few glugs of olive oil
1 onion finely chopped
1 stick of celery finely chopped
300g risotto/arborio rice (serves 3-4)
1 glass white wine/sherry/madeira
1 litre stock
Wild garlic pesto

METHOD

1. Place the oil in a pan and heat slightly.
2. Fry the chopped onion and celery for a minute or two to start the softening process.
3. Add the risotto rice and fry for 1-2 minutes until you can see the rice start to change colour and go slightly translucent.
4. Add the glass of wine and mix in (optional).
5. Slowly start to add the stock about a ladle-full at a time and stir in as you go until each ladle seems to be absorbed. Take your time – it should take you at least 10 minutes to do this.
6. The knack with risotto is to work the rice almost like massaging it rather than stirring it.

7. Keep going until all the stock is used up – you may need to add more or less depending on your rice.

8. Keep stirring and tasting it until it feels like it is about 80% cooked.

9. At this point put a lid on for a minute, then turn the heat off.

10. DO NOT OPEN THE LID.

11. Wait about 10 minutes for the rice to finish cooking.

12. When done, serve in bowls with crusty bread and a large dollop of wild garlic pesto.

Index

A
almonds 21
anchovy 26
apple 11, 14, 16
artichoke 41
avocado 27, 54, 55, 57

B
bagel 37
baguette 33
basil 26
beans 8, 41, 54, 55
bread 8, 17, 28, 33, 35, 47, 51, 57, 63
broccoli 8

C
capers 26, 39, 41
carrot 8, 28
celery 28, 62
cheese 23, 29, 37, 46, 53
chicken 23
chickpeas 28
chilli 25-27, 54
chips 11, 24, 25
coddler 52, 53
coriander 25, 54, 55
corn 24, 25
cream 29, 37
cucumber 28, 37, 40

D
dandelioin 3
dill 14, 15
doughballs 9
dressing 8, 10, 11, 16, 41

E
egg 10, 23, 35, 38, 39, 41, 44, 49, 51-55, 57

F
fish 9, 10
flour 44
flower 2-4, 5 14, 15

G
garlic 1-5, 8-11, 13, 14, 16, 17, 21, 23-29, 33, 35, 37-41, 44-47, 49, 51, 53-55, 57-63
gherkins 26
guacamole 27

H
ham 23, 37
hazelnuts 21
hummus 23, 28, 37

K
ketchup 24

L
lime 25, 27

M
madeira 62
mayonnaise 10, 35, 39
milk 44
mint 26
mozzarella 59
Mushroom 44, 46
mushrooms 44, 45
mustard 14-16

N
nutmeg 56
nuts 21

O
oil 8, 16, 21, 25-28, 40, 44, 45, 47, 49, 53-55, 59, 60, 62
olive oil 8, 16, 21, 25-28, 40, 44, 45, 47, 49, 55, 59, 60, 62
olives 41
omelette 49
onion 3, 24, 25, 44, 45, 47, 54, 55, 62
orange 5

P
pancake 44-46, 49
paprika 54, 55
parmesan 21
pasta 54, 59
pepper 16, 39, 47, 54, 55, 57, 60
peppers 54, 55
pesto 21, 23, 29, 33, 37, 38, 47, 56-63
pickled 40, 41
pitta 28, 47
pizza 8, 10
potato 9, 10, 23, 39, 41, 47, 56

Q
quiche 39

R
rice 23, 60-63
ricotta 29
risotto 8, 9, 23, 33, 62
rocket 40

S
salad 8, 10, 11, 16, 17, 39-41, 49, 59
salmon 23, 26, 29, 37, 41, 60, 61
salsa 24, 26, 27, 55
sandwich 10, 23, 35, 37, 57
sausage 54
seeds 2, 4, 5, 14, 15, 2140
sherry 62
Sourdough 51
spaghetti 23, 59
steak 26, 60

T
tacos 25
tomato 24, 25, 26, 27, 40, 41, 54, 55, 57, 59
tortilla 24, 25, 54, 55

V
Vinaigrette 16
vinegar 8, 11, 14-17, 26

Printed in Great Britain
by Amazon